Saxophone Surprise

by Sydnie Meltzer Kleinhenz

illustrated by Esther Szegedy

Scott Foresman

Editorial Offices: Glenview, Illinois • New York, New York
Sales Offices: Reading, Massachusetts • Duluth, Georgia
Glenview, Illinois • Carrollton, Texas • Menlo Park, California

Sam flopped on his bed.

"I panicked at that talent show," he moaned. "My saxophone just honked and beeped. At recess, the kids laughed and called me 'saxophone goose.'"

"Only a silly goose listens to that," said Kyle. "You're good at playing sax. You've been in the orchestra for years."

Sam sat up. "In orchestra other kids are playing too. But in the recital I'll be playing all alone. I wish I were a big basketball star like you. People treat you like a king."

Kyle played a make-believe violin. "What a sad story," he said. "Listen. I get nervous too. To relax, I think about basketball. I try to see only the hoop."

Sam was quiet. "Big brothers are supposed to know what to do," he said. "Thanks."

Kyle had a practice game that day. Sam went to watch.

Kyle closed his eyes and blew out a big breath. He squinted. Sam could tell he was trying to see only the hoop. Then Kyle threw the ball.

"Way to go!" yelled the coach.

Sam clapped and hooted. He couldn't wait to cheer for Kyle at Saturday's game.

Kyle gave Sam a wink.

Sam waved as he left for his sax lesson.

Mr. Lott welcomed Sam.

"We're going to have a real rehearsal today," he said. "My neighbors will be the audience."

Sam nodded. His throat got tight.

"It's just a rehearsal," he told himself. "Just relax."

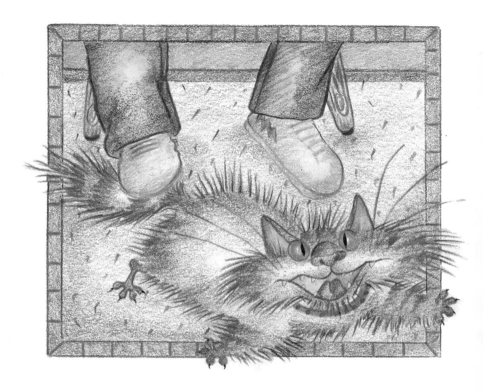

Sam closed his eyes. He blew out a big breath. He squinted until he saw only the notes on the page. He didn't see the cat. The cat leaped right onto Miss Peel. Miss Peel screeched. She spilled lemonade on Mr. Rafe's foot.

"I'm sorry. I'm sorry," said Sam.

"Rehearsal is over," muttered Mr. Lott as he wiped up lemonade.

9

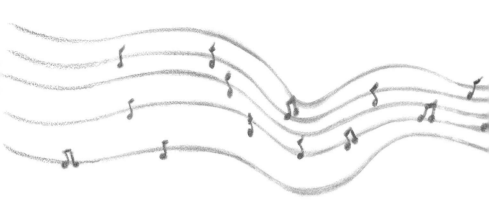

Sam's mom met him at the door. "Mr. Lott called. He wants you to have a rehearsal here at home," she said. "Tonight."

Sam looked for Kyle. "Help! I need a new way to relax."

Kyle thought a moment. "I read about a singer. She pretends everyone is a baby. Then they seem silly and she doesn't get nervous."

Everyone waited. Sam played a few measures. His throat got tight. He blew harder. Honk! Beep!

"Relax!" he said to himself.

Sam peeked over the music. He imagined Dad as a baby.

Suddenly everyone looked like a baby.

Sam played a few more measures. Then he burst into laughter. He laughed so hard he fell to the floor. Mom frowned and ended the rehearsal. Then it wasn't so funny anymore.

Sam woke up early on Saturday. He couldn't wait to cheer at Kyle's game. But he dreaded the recital. His throat felt so tight that his words came out in croaks and whispers. How would Kyle hear him cheer?

Sam knew! He grabbed his sax and ran.

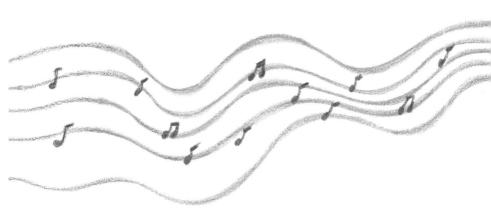

At the game, Sam played a tune that said it all. "Tah-dah-dah-dot, dah-dah!" People yelled, "Charge!" They clapped and smiled.

Kyle heard the sax. He gave Sam a wink. Then he closed his eyes and blew out a big breath. He looked at the hoop. *Swish!* Another point!

The coach waved his arms like a conductor
with an orchestra. Sam played, "Tah-dah-dah-
dot, dah-dah!" He led the cheering crowd for
the whole game.

After the game, Kyle patted Sam on the back. "You played so well for that big audience."

Sam's eyes widened in surprise. He had! He nodded slowly.

"Tah-dah-dah-dot, dah-dah!" sang Kyle.

"Charge!" croaked a happy Sam. Right then, he knew he could do it. He headed home to get ready for that recital.